We Can All Paint!

Written by
Jill Atkins

It is fun to paint.

You can get in such a mess if you like.

Gail painted her hands.

Then she did a sheet of hand art.

Padma painted her hands with henna. It looks so good!

Flick has painted nails.

Some of them are painted red. Some of them have little spots.

You can paint with a brush.

Ella painted with a thin brush.

Fred painted with a thick brush.

Ana painted on bricks.

She needed a brush and paints. Then she started to paint.

Then it was finished. Ana stood back and looked at it.

Did she like it?
I think she did!

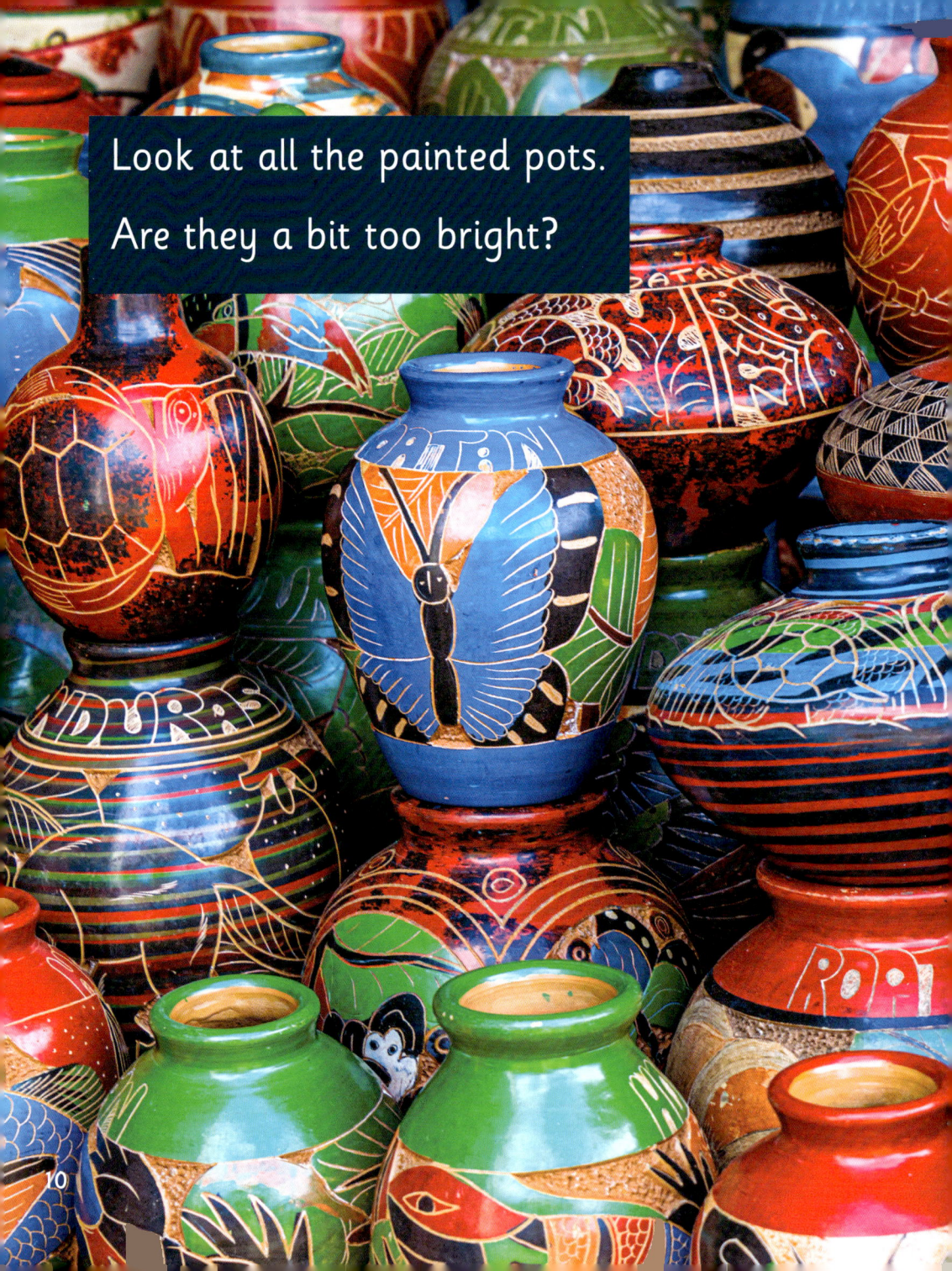

Look at all the painted pots.
Are they a bit too bright?

One man painted this cup.

Do you like it?
Or do you think it is a mess?

This is an artist.

She has painted a river and some trees.

Do you think she can paint well?

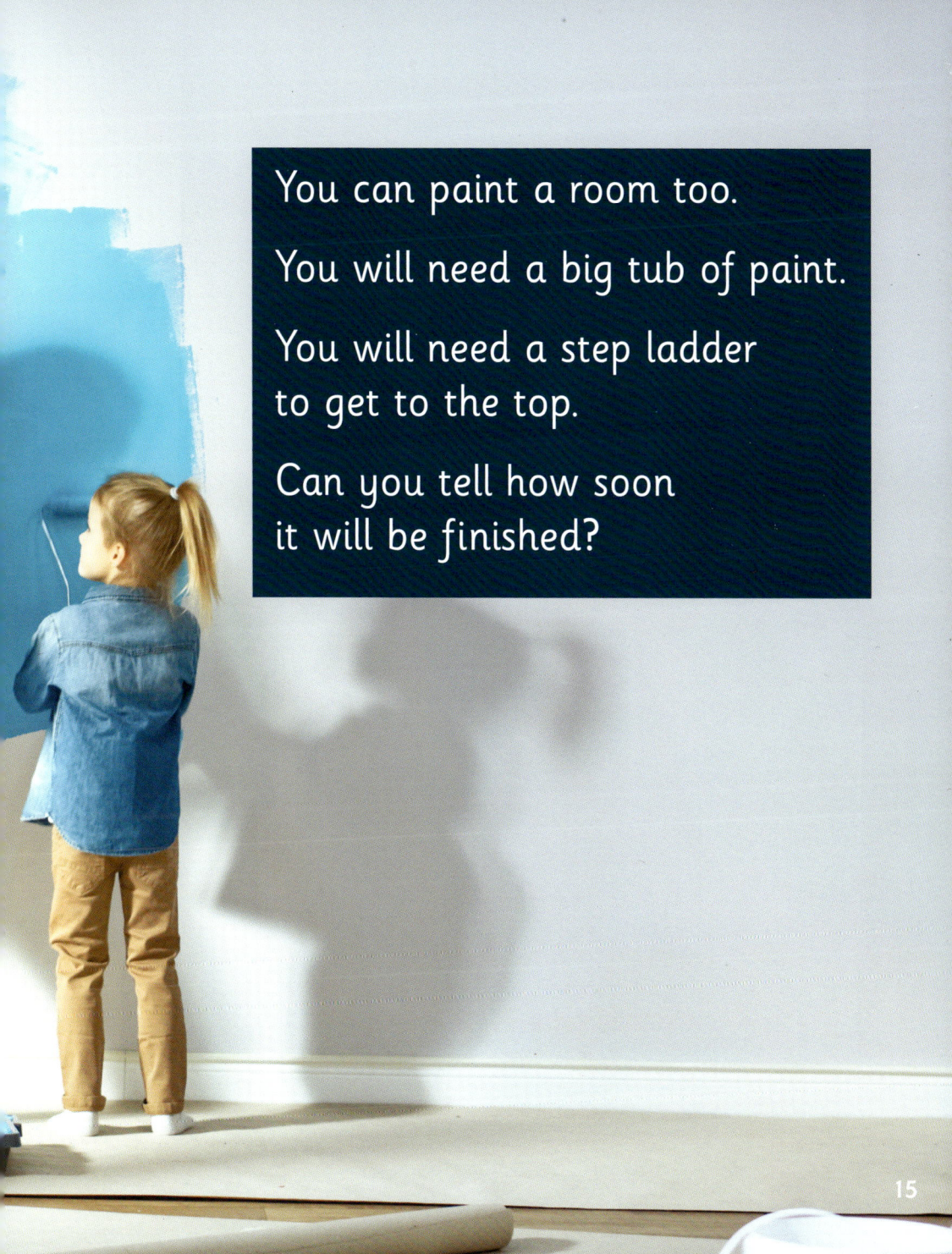

You can paint a room too.

You will need a big tub of paint.

You will need a step ladder to get to the top.

Can you tell how soon it will be finished?

All sorts of things can be painted.

Look at some of them.